IMAGES OF ENGLAND

Abbeydale
& Millhouses

Abbeydale House. M558/

John Rodgers, for many years head of the world famous cutlery firm Joseph Rodgers and Sons Ltd, built Abbeydale House around 1850 and lived in it until his death in 1859. When the house was auctioned a year later with a large area of land around it, the auction notice was almost breathless in its praise. 'First class mansion and pleasure grounds' it said, built regardless of expense in the Italian style of architecture, 'situate in one of the most favourable sites in the far-framed valley of the Sheaf, commanding beautiful and extensive views over the surrounding country, which is richly wooded and highly picturesque'. It described at length the various rooms: dining room, drawing room, library, boudoir, entrance hall, central hall, servants' hall, housekeeper's room, butler's pantry, six bedrooms, and concluded, 'Abbeydale House, in situation, character and extent, forms a most desirable residence for a family of the highest respectability and position'. The house was later owned by John Firth. It is still standing in the 1990s but no longer looks as grand as this. The building is run down, garden, wall, railings and trees have gone and a block of red brick shops, built on the front of the house, prevent it being seen from the main road.

IMAGES OF ENGLAND

Abbeydale
& Millhouses

Peter Harvey

NONSUCH

First published 1996
This new pocket edition 2005
Images unchanged from first edition

Nonsuch Publishing Limited
The Mill, Brimscombe Port,
Stroud, Gloucestershire, GL5 2QG
www.nonsuch-publishing.com

British Library Cataloguing in Publication Data.
A catalogue record for this book is available from the British Library.

ISBN 1-84588-124-9

Typesetting and origination by Nonsuch Publishing Limited
Printed in Great Britain by Oaklands Book Services Limited

Contents

Acknowledgements

Old photographs, and even those that are not so old, are precious to the people who own them. For their trust in allowing me to borrow photographs, for help in acquiring them, or for information about them, my grateful thanks to Peter Charlton, editor of *The Star*, Sylvia Pybus and her colleagues in Sheffield Local Studies Library, David Sempers, chairman of Abbey Glen Laundry, Tim Carrington, managing director of Loxleys, Charles Hall, Bob Jackson, Raymond Morris, Bert Dagg, George Greaves, Derek Doman, Mike Gent, Ann Slater, Brian Carr, Jane and John Harrod, Simon Heath-Harvey, Sarah Hough, Norman Bradbury, H.B. Priestley, E.H. Tomlin, Mary Elliott, Peter and Rachel Cranwell, Rosemary Ward, Horace Clayton, Pat and Doug Spence, Darrell Stent, Yorkshire Co-operatives Ltd. and the gentleman who, many months ago, gave me a copy of the old photograph of Millhouses police. I kept his name on a bit of paper. Unfortunately, whereas I am extremely careful with old photographs, I am lamentably careless with bits of paper. My apologies in advance to anybody else I have missed out. If there are mistakes in this book they are not the responsibility of any of the people mentioned above. They are mine.

Introduction

Abbeydale is a difficult area to define. The old Abbeydale Cinema is a long way from Abbeydale Park, or Abbeydale golf course. On one side, Abbeydale soon blurs into Sharrow or Nether Edge; on the other, it just as soon becomes Heeley or Woodseats. On its way out of town it passes through the areas of Millhouses and Beauchief and stretches almost to Dore or Totley Brook. The late Mary Walton, a local historian whose knowledge of Sheffield was vast, had a try at defining Abbeydale in one of her books. It was virtually the valley of the River Sheaf, she said, stretching from Heeley Bridge to Dore Road. For the purposes of this book I have gone a little way past Dore Road to include Abbeydale Park and Abbeydale Hall, but everything else falls within Mary Walton's definition.

Modern Abbeydale owes its existence, firstly, to the old Baslow turnpike road, built in 1805. Before that there were only fields, narrow tracks, farms dotted about the landscape, mills and wheels scattered along the River Sheaf and small groups of cottages here and there. The effect of the turnpike was not immediate. Inns were built to sustain travellers but even by the 1860s, Abbeydale was still largely countryside. The first houses were gentlemen's country residences: Chipping House, Abbeydale House, Abbeydale Grange, Gatefield, Abbeydale Hall. It was not until the second half of the nineteenth century that housing began to spread along the old turnpike road and by then another important influence had appeared: the Midland Railway line from Sheffield to Chesterfield which opened on 1 February 1870 and gave Sheffield its first direct main line link with London.

The new railway line provided Abbeydale with three suburban stations, at Millhouses, Beauchief and Dore and Totley, but more importantly, it attracted factories and workshops along the way for firms who wanted sidings on which to receive their raw materials and send out their products, especially on a direct line to London. The factories needed a workforce and the workforce needed houses, shops, schools, churches and places of entertainment. There is a rough guide to the outward spread of housing along Abbeydale Road at this time from the few houses which have the year they were built carved into their frontage: 1879 on a terrace at the Highfield end, 1884 on another group beyond that, 1891 on a house near the old Abbeydale Cinema. The Lake District houses at the bottom of Woodseats Road have no dates on them but they too fit into the pattern. They were built in 1897.

The first large scale housing scheme at Millhouses was in 1875 when the Oakdale Estate was developed around Knaresborough, Sterndale and Hartington Roads. Before that, Millhouses was a small and fairly remote hamlet on the fringe of the town. Apart from the Oakdale development, housing was built slowly and piecemeal at Millhouses and it was not until the mid 1920s that the red brick semis started to appear. By then, the outer half of Abbeydale was emerging as a playground area for people from all over the city. They were attracted by large areas of woodland, sports pitches, golf courses and, most of all, by Millhouses Park.

Earl Fitzwilliam, the largest landowner in the area, gave the city a small piece of land in the valley bottom in 1907 and suggested that it should become a public park. The City Council bought more land and the park that eventually built covered thirty-one acres and stretched for a mile, from Archer Road almost to Abbey Lane. By the 1930s it had a cricket ground, open areas, tennis courts, bowling greens, children's paddling pools, a boating pond, flower gardens, extensive paths and an open air swimming pool that ultimately became a lido. In the 1960s and 1970s when Sheffield had cheap bus fares, it was not unusual for 50,000 people to use the park over a warm, sunny weekend. Some of them came from places far outside Sheffield. They had seen the park as they passed by on a train, admired it, and returned for a closer look.

For anybody who remembers those times, walking through the park in the 1990s is a saddening experience. The old pavilion near the tennis courts was badly damaged in a fire and was not rebuilt. The lido closed and the site it occupied is now four feet high in weeds. The River Sheaf is contaminated, smells, and there are notices posted along its banks warning that children should not paddle or bathe in it. The paddling pools need repair and are closed. The boating pond is closed because of the shortage of water. The footpaths are crumbling. There is a depressing feeling around that the 'temporary' closure of the paddling pools and boating pond might well become permanent. Millhouses Park no longer attracts 50,000 people on a warm weekend. Those who say that nostalgia is wasteful and pointless are wrong in this respect: it is only by looking back at what the park used to be that we realise how urgently it needs work doing on it today.

Publication of this book is timely as far as Millhouses is concerned. In 1996 more building work is going on, or in prospect, in the area than ever before. Sainsbury's store on Archer Road is being extended with more car parking and a new access road. There are plans for a family health and fitness centre alongside the store with an indoor swimming pool, fitness studio, steam rooms, saunas, lounge bar and restaurant. A new car showroom is nearing completion on the opposite side of Archer Road. A new Tesco store is being built on the other side of the railway line with an access road off Abbeydale Road. A new filling station is being built opposite Grange School. A three-storey block of old people's retirement flats is well advanced on what used to be the old tram loop at Terminus Road. Sheffield United FC have plans to develop a football centre of excellence at Grange School.

Change is all around.

One

Abbeydale Road

Herschell Road was built off Abbeydale Road in the 1880s and named after Sir Frederick William Herschell, the astronomer. By the time this photograph was taken by John William Mottershaw in the early 1900s, it was well settled, with Swan's grocery store on one corner of its junction with Abbeydale Road and W. White, butcher, on the other.

Abbeydale P.M. Chapel. M&S. 228.

Above: Abbeydale Primitive Methodist church, at the bottom of South View Road, came about through the efforts of a man with the unusual name of Hosea Tugby, who lived and owned property in Abbeydale Road area in the 1880s. He started a mission which met over a stable in Sellers Street, then decided to build a permanent church which opened on 29 August 1891. In 1949, the building was sold and became a Christian Science church.

Left: Ada Bond standing outside Tom Bond's grocery at No. 603 Abbeydale Road, in about 1930.

Abbeydale Road, Sheffield. No. 2795.

Above: Abbeydale Road, looking towards Chippinghouse Road and South View Road junctions, had one motor car, one van and a cyclist in it when this photograph was taken in the early 1920s. In the 1990s there are times when this stretch of road is so crowded with traffic it is difficult for pedestrians to cross. The houses on the right lost their wrought-iron railings for scrap during the Second World War.

Right: There seems to have been an unusual mixture of activities at Bannerdale Fruit Stores, Abbeydale Road, at the time this picture was taken in the 1920s. The proprietor, J. Bothamley, is described on the front window as fruiterer and coal merchant.

Abbeydale Cinema opened on 20 December 1920 with a film called *The Call of the Road*. It was one of Sheffield's largest suburban cinemas, with seating for 1,560, a café at balcony level, a ballroom and billiard hall in the basement and facilities for putting on stage shows. It closed on 5 July 1975, three days after this photograph was taken. For several years the main building was used as office equipment showrooms. The basement is still in business as a snooker hall and bar but the cinema part of the building has stood empty since the office equipment showrooms closed in 1991 and its future is undecided.

Right: The cinema's forthcoming attractions leaflet for August 1974 included Tom Baker in *The Golden Voyage of Sinbad*, Bruce Lee in *Way of the Dragon*, Helen Hayes and Stephanie Powers in *Herbie Rides Again* and Paul Newman, Robert Redford and Robert Shaw in *The Sting.*

Below: St Peter's church, Abbeydale, seen here in about 1904, was built to replace a temporary iron mission church at Rufford Road and consecrated by the Archbishop of York on 5 June 1895. The old iron mission church was taken down and rebuilt on a new site adjoining the church where it served as a church hall up to 1961.

AUGUST, 1974
Programmes Subject To Alteration

ST PETERS, SHEFFIELD.   F.K. 625. S.

13

A new church hall, built alongside St Peter's church, Abbeydale, was opened by the Assistant Bishop of Sheffield, the Rt Revd G.V. Gerard, in April 1962.

Abbeydale Road, Sheffield. No. 1547.

Abbeydale Cinema had not been open long when this photograph was taken in the early 1920s from the Abbeydale Road and Broadfield Road junction. Since then, the buildings on the left have stayed pretty much the same but those on the right, the newsagent's shop and all the houses as far back as Bedale Road, have been demolished. A car showroom was built on part of the site and the rest was grassed and planted with trees.

The swimming baths on Broadfield Road are a stone's throw from the rear of the Abbeydale Cinema and a 100 yard walk from Abbeydale Road, but they have always been called Heeley Baths rather than Abbeydale Baths. They were built on what was originally known as Primrose Meadows and opened in July 1909. In the early days, charges at the baths were 4d on clean water days (of which there were two a week) and 2d and 1d on other days.

Like all turnpike roads, Abbeydale Road had its toll bar, the Broadfield toll bar, sometimes called Abbeydale Road toll bar, which stood on land between what is now Hale Street and the old Abbeydale Cinema. The bar closed in 1873. This painting, signed 'H. Smith', is dated 1880 and was probably done to mark the closure of the remaining toll bars on the Baslow turnpike on 1 November that year.

Sheldon Rd, M8S.

BROADFIELD HOTEL
ALBERT TWIGG.

Old Lodge Abbeydale. —JW

Sheldon Lodge stood in Abbeydale Road, near the bottom of Sheldon Road, until it was demolished in the early 1900s. For more than thirty years it was the home of Mrs Elizabeth Fox, who is standing by the railings in this photograph.

Opposite above: Sheldon Road, pictured around 1904, has a sedate look to it, with every window decorously curtained and not a vehicle of any kind in sight. The road surface leaves something to be desired, however. It certainly wouldn't do for the volume of traffic using it today. The road was built in 1880 on land owned by the Sheldon family.

Opposite below: The Broadfield Hotel as it was in 1900, when Albert Twigg was landlord. The building to the left is Abbeydale Road Board School which was opened on 27 October 1890 and is still there today, as Abbeydale Primary School.

Parts of Abbeydale have always been prone to flooding during extremely heavy rain, but this particular flood on Abbeydale Road in October 1989 had nothing to do with the weather. It was caused by a burst water main. The worst affected houses and shops were in the dip between Gatefield Road and Marden Road.

Opposite above: It was story time when these children at Abbeydale Primary School were photographed in July 1968. Since then the school has celebrated its centenary. Its official opening, by J.D. Leader, former proprietor of the Sheffield and Rotherham Independent, was on 27 November 1890.

Opposite below: Glen Road, seen here in the 1920s, is older than most of the other offshoots from Abbeydale Road. The top part of it was built in 1865 as part of a development carried out by the Montgomery Freehold Land Society. The houses shown here at the bottom of the road were built later.

There are twenty-four people in this 1916 view of Carter Knowle Road, and most of them are children. Six of them are on the pavement. All the others are standing, walking, or in one case cycling, on the road. One of the boys, with his cap, apron and basket, looks like a delivery boy. Jay walkers and delivery boys are much rarer on Carter Knowle Road today.

Carter Knowle Road again, but photographed a year or two earlier. The houses on either side of the road have not changed a great deal in eighty years, but the trees are much bigger.

Above: Carter Knowle Council School was built at the corner of Carter Knowle Road and Bannerdale Road and opened in January 1906. When this photograph was taken, around the time of its opening, the paving stones outside the school wall were still being laid.

Right: The old penny farthing bicycle above Butterworth's cycle shop at the corner of Abbeydale Road and Leyburn Road has been in place for about fifty years. The shop was set up in 1932 by Albert Edward Butterworth and is still in the same family. His grandson, Matthew Butterworth, ran it in the 1990s. The penny farthing was hoisted above the shop in the mid 1940s.

Archer Lane

Throughout the 1880s and 1890s new houses were built along Abbeydale Road at a fast rate, although for many years it was still possible to walk a few hundred yards off the main road and find a surprisingly rural scene. Archer Lane, pictured here, is the best example.

A few houses were built around Archer Lane in the 1930s but it was not until the late 1950s, when a start was made on the Knab Farm Estate, that the the area was extensively developed.

Jennings Farm, near Archer Lane, photographed from Brincliffe Edge Road before its outbuildings were demolished in the early 1900s. The house survived and is still there. Most of the land around it was built on in the 1930s and 1960s.

Much of the land attached to Abbeydale House was used for house building in 1897. The houses that were built became known as the Lake District, or the Lakes, because the streets were all named after towns, lakes, or other features in the English Lake District: Arnside, Crummock, Coniston, Grasmere, Keswick and others. Buttermere Road was photographed in 1945 as residents put out their flags and bunting to celebrate VE Day, Victory in Europe.

Abbeydale Road, photographed in about 1904 from the bottom of Woodseats Road, with an open top tram car in the distance on its way back to town. At this time all the buildings on the right hand side were private houses.

Abbeydale Road, photographed ten or fifteen years later from roughly the same place. The houses on both corners of Grasmere Road and some of the houses lower down have become shops. One of the shops on Grasmere Road corner is Shentall's, the grocers.

Falling advertising hoardings are not a common traffic hazard in the Abbeydale area but this unlucky motorist encountered some in December 1982 when he was driving down the bottom of Woodseats Road. During a day of gales, a strong gust blew the hoardings down on top of his car. Fortunately he was not injured.

Abbeydale Road has been best known in the last twenty years for its antique, curio, secondhand and collectors' shops which attract collectors and dealers from all over the country and from abroad. These are just three of them. At the time of writing there are seventeen more, plus a large antiques emporium in nearby Broadfield Road with more than fifty dealers.

Two

Millhouses

Holt House cottages, with their stone roofs, shuttered windows and whitewashed walls, have an English village look about them. They stood at the corner of Abbeydale Road and Bannerdale Road, roughly where Holt House School is today.

Holt House was an old farm rather than a gentleman's residence. In the 1841 Sheffield Directory, when George Wragg was farmer there, it is listed as Hoult House but by the 1850s and '60s it had become Holt House. The farm disappeared many years ago and Holt House Infants School was built on part of its land.

Because it was built near to the ancient border between Mercia and Northumbria, St Oswald's church, Millhouses, was dedicated to King Oswald, who restored the Christian religion to Northumbria. The site for the church, at the corner of Abbeydale Road and Bannerdale Road, was given by Thomas Firth and the foundation stone was laid by Mrs Firth on 22 March 1909. She is the lady with her back to the camera in the centre of the picture. The church was dedicated by Archbishop Lang on 4 July 1910 and consecrated by him on 31 October 1914.

Above: Boys of the 35th Sheffield (St Oswald's) cubs were photographed at Thorpe Hesley in 1986 during celebrations to mark the 70th anniversary of the foundation of the cubs.

Right: St Oswald's church, Millhouses, seen from Abbeydale Road in 1959.

Abbeydale Grange was once the home of Sir Wilson Mappin, director of the Sheffield Gas Company from 1885 to 1918, and its chairman for several years. Unlike his father, Sir Frederick Thorpe Mappin, MP, former Master Cutler, former Mayor of Sheffield and Freeman of the town, Sir Wilson took no part in public or political affairs but he was well known as a philanthropist. His home later became a school.

Opposite above: The Grange was empty and partly boarded up when it was badly damaged by fire in July 1994. Not long after, to the dismay of conservationists, the old building was demolished.

Opposite below: Abbeydale Road, with the grounds of Holt House to the left, Troutbeck Road going off to the right and beyond that, Archer Road. The trees on the left of the picture are still there but those on the right were chopped down because they were a traffic hazard.

Abbeydale Rd Millhouses. M&S.

Nowadays this is the last stretch of Abbeydale Road going out of the city. Originally the road had the same name all the way out to Totley Brook, but by the 1890s house numbers were well into the 900s. To avoid them going over 1,000, the section of Abbeydale Road from Millhouses Lane to Totley Brook was renamed Abbeydale Road South.

Nestling in the hollow between Abbeydale Road and the old locomotive shed, Moscar Cottages, photographed here around 1905, must have been ideal homes for Edwardian train spotters. There are still houses in the hollow but they are no longer as secluded as this. The area was transformed in the 1990s by building work for a new supermarket, its access road and parking area.

The cottages, seen here from another angle, were built in 1859 near the old Moscar grinding wheel. Part of the old wheel dam can be seen on the picture. On the right is a corner of the locomotive shed.

Abbeydale Grange School, at the junction of Abbeydale Road and Hastings Road, opened on 9 September 1958 as Abbeydale Grammar School for Boys. The official opening, on 23 July 1959, was performed by James Chuter Ede, former Home Secretary (1945–1951) and later Baron Chuter-Ede of Epsom. It ceased to be a grammar school in the change-over to comprehensive education.

The road across Millhouses railway bridge was originally called Station Road because it led to the old Millhouses and Ecclesall railway station, seen here in the foreground, with its booking office entrance on the bridge. Once over the bridge the road divided into what were little more than cart tracks. In 1906 it was renamed Archer Road.

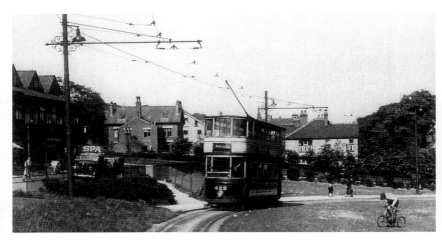

There are three points of interest in this photograph: the old tramcar on Millhouses terminus loop, the Spa mineral waters delivery lorry on Terminus Road and the small boy on a vintage three wheel bike, out of the saddle as he toils up the grassy bank.

Woodend Farm stood on part of what later became the Laycock Engineering Ltd site in Archer Road. The Midland railway line can just be made out, top right, at the back of the farmhouse. The building immediately behind the farm has the look of a railway building. In the years before the Second World War the Gyte Brothers had the farm.

The building behind Woodend Farm in the top picture survived after the farm had been demolished. It was still there in 1992. Painted on one wall was a sign saying 'Air Raid Shelter Number 7' and an arrow pointing down steps leading under the building, which gives a clue to its use during the Second World War. At that time the site was in use as a car scrapyard and the old building was one of the few left standing. Since then it has been demolished to make way for extensions to the nearby Sainsbury's store.

The Millhouses Hotel, as it was in the 1950s. The building on the right was demolished some years later to make space for the pub carpark.

Millhouses shopping area in the 1930s, with Archer Road going off to the right. Buildings on both sides of Abbeydale Road nearest to the camera were destroyed or badly damaged by bombing in the Second World War. Those on the left were replaced by new shops built at an angle across the Springfield Road corner. Those on the right were rebuilt and set back. Old fashioned Belisha beacons mark the pedestrian crossings of both Abbeydale and Archer Roads.

The start of Abbeydale Road South, from Archer Road, as it looked in the 1930s. The shop on the corner of Archer Road was a grocers at the time, hence the window sign, 'Finest quality tinned goods. A large variety'. In the 1990s it became a bistro. The shop on the opposite side, at the Whirlowdale Road corner, started as a fruit shop but by the time this picture was taken it was Hobson's chemist and druggist. The old style chemist's weighing machine can just be seen on the shop front.

Springfield Road looking towards Millhouses, around 1909.

Springfield Road looking towards Ecclesall in the 1930s. The most obvious difference between these two photographs is the way that the planting of trees in front gardens softened the view.

Millhouses Lane is one of the oldest roads in the area, although it was originally no more than a narrow track. Even in the early 1900s when this photograph was taken looking towards Millhouses, it had the appearance of a small country road.

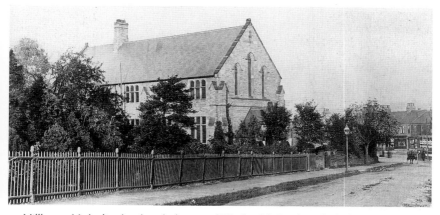

Millhouses Methodist church at the bottom of Whirlowdale Road as it looked in 1905, not long after it was built. It was enlarged in the 1930s to the corner of Whirlowdale Road and Millhouses Lane. The new part of the building, including a spire which became a well known Millhouses landmark, was opened on 21 May 1936.

The Robin Hood Hotel, at the bottom of Millhouses Lane, was a small country pub when it was photographed here in 1902. When it was offered for sale in 1863 it was described as 'an old licensed inn known by the sign of the Robin Hood and Little John'. Just how old is unsure, but it was certainly listed in the 1841 Directory. The hotel has been substantially enlarged at the rear but happily, the old frontage is still recognisable.

One's first reaction to this photograph of Millhouses division policemen, taken in the 1890s, is that twenty-seven seems to be rather a lot of them for a small and relatively peaceful area like Millhouses. The reason there were so many is that the division covered a very large area, stretching to Dore, Ringinglow, Hunter's Bar, Sharrowvale and Brincliffe Edge Road. When the division was set up in 1893, Police Constable Smith, who had been stationed at Millhouses for some years, was promoted to sergeant and lived in the house attached to the new police station. He is probably one of the two sergeants on the picture.

Millhouses was not the centre of a police division for very long and when the police station in Archer Road built in 1893 was no longer needed, it was taken over by the Parks Department. It was used as the Millhouses Park Keeper's house and became known as Park Lodge. In recent years it has been used as a store.

Right: Watched by more than 2,000 people, the highest structure in Millhouses, a 190 ft high chimney on Archer Road, was knocked down in 1983 to make way for a new Sainsbury's supermarket. The chimney, at a former brickworks, had been a landmark in the area for thirty years. The charges to bring it down were set off by Mary Williamson of Bakewell, daughter of the steeplejack who built it, Jack Lister.

Below: Many of the houses on Hartington Road (above), Knaresborough Road, Sterndale Road, and some at the bottom of Whirlowdale Road, were built by a freehold land society as part of what was called the Oakdale Estate, Millhouses. The society was established in 1875 to buy the estate, build roads and divide the land into sixty allotments for the building of houses. One of its rules was that the houses should have stone fronts and sides, but bricks could be used at the rear, which is how they were built.

Holy Trinity, Millhouses.

Above: The first church to be built on Grove Road, Millhouses, was this one, built at a cost of £2,000 in the 1890s as a chapel of ease for Ecclesall church and known as Holy Trinity Mission Room. The Archbishop of York preached at the first service on 13 November 1897. Photographs of the old building are very hard to find. This architect's drawing is dated 1895.

Left: The old church on Grove Road eventually became a mission church to St Oswald's, then, when a new parish was created, it was demolished and the present Holy Trinity was built on the site. The foundation stone was laid by the Revd Alfred Wood, first vicar of the new parish, on 4 January 1936 and the building was completed the following year.

Farmland still separates Millhouses and Ecclesall on this late 1930s aerial photograph. Ecclesall Woods are on the left of the picture, with Endowood Road and Whirlowdale Crescent running alongside. Millhouses Park, sandwiched between Abbeydale Road South and the Sheffield-St Pancras railway line, is an obvious feature and still has its old oblong-shaped open air swimming pool. Housing has not yet spread very far up the hill towards Ecclesall. Dobcroft Road is undeveloped beyond Whirlowdale Crescent, Whirlowdale Road has only four houses between Dobcroft Road and Endowood Road, and Millhouses Lane still has fields alongside much of its middle section. The houses at the bottom right are on Dalewood Road and Dalewood Avenue.

An attractive feature of the old Millhouses tram terminus when it was first built was the tram stop shelter which can be seen on the left of this 1950s photograph. It had wooden seating round the inside for waiting passengers and there were discreetly placed public conveniences attached on either side. It looked like the sort of building that would not have been out of place in a seaside resort.

In later years the old tram shelter was a target for vandals and was badly in need of repair. The wooden seats were smashed and eventually removed, the walls were covered with graffiti, the roof leaked, some of the windows were boarded up because of repeated damage and the public conveniences were closed in a bout of council cost-cutting. On the morning of 11 December 1994 a bulldozer moved in and by lunch time the shelter had gone.

Another attractive feature of the area was the patch of green in the middle of the old tram loop, with its flowering cherry trees. On 16 May 1996 a bulldozer arrived and the trees were ripped out just as they were in full flower. Soon after, work started on the building of a three storey block of retirement flats on the site.

By August 1996 a giant crane was on the site and the flats were already up to the second storey. A modern, one-sided bus shelter had replaced the old red brick tram shelter and the flowering cherry trees were no more than a memory.

The Waggon and Horses, Millhouses, in its early 1900s state with outhouses to the right and Joseph H. Marshall as landlord. Judging by the roof levels and the different sized stones, the windowless section to the left of the building was a nineteenth-century extension.

Tea rooms were built alongside the Waggon and Horses in 1920 and this picture was taken soon after they opened. Land on the opposite side of the road was still under cultivation. Within ten years it was covered with new houses, shops and streets.

A waggon and horse outside the Waggon and Horses. It seems to be an early 1900s delivery of provisions of some kind with a lady on the far side in the process of making a purchase from the bowler-hatted tradesman. This entrance to the pub was blocked off when it was revamped in the 1990s.

By 1974 when this photograph was taken, the Waggon and Horses and its neighbouring tea rooms had been joined to make one building. It was used here as a background when members of Sheffield Dickens Fellowship posed with the 1830s-vintage Gay Gordons coach for a picture intended for the front cover of a Christmas edition of the magazine *Yorkshire Life*. The coach came from Darley Dale School of Equitation and the two Dickens Fellowship members in the foreground were Arthur Brookes, president, and Joyce Dale, secretary.

An unidentified wedding group photographed at the rear of the Waggon and Horses, around 1930.

Abbeydale Rd. Millhouses. M&S 150B.

There are some bends and twists in the road here that will be unfamiliar to modern eyes. It was Abbeydale Road; it is now Abbeydale Road South and the building on the right is the Waggon and Horses public house. In later years land on both sides was taken to straighten the road. When the picture was taken, the Waggon had an orchard at the side where the tea rooms were later built.

Pingle Avenue, Millhouses

Pingle Avenue, Millhouses, in the 1930s. Many of the houses in this area were built during the 1920s by Tom Henry Bailey. One old resident told me several years ago that when the houses were being built, people often called at the site to see Mr Bailey. If he was at his house in Whirlowdale Road, the workmen would say, 'he's up yonda'. So Mr Bailey named his house Yonda. I don't know how true the story is, but there is certainly a house on Whirlowdale Road called Yonda.

The grass verge alongside Abbeydale Road South from Archer Road up to the Waggon and Horses, used to be well known for its groups of large trees, but in recent years they have been drastically thinned. Of the five shown on this late 1980s photograph, only one is still standing and the tree on the other side of the privet hedge, in Millhouses Park, has also been chopped down.

Dobcroft Middle School at the top of Pingle Road, Millhouses, opened on 6 March 1970. It was considered unusual at the time for its open plan design which broke away from the formal classroom layout.

Dobcroft Middle School's M3 and M4 years, photographed in 1975, include: Deborah Seemley, Katrina Pass, Judith Porter, Rachel Gomery, Karen Alexander, Shanet Alexander, Jane Barker, Anne Crapper, Jane Barrett, Regan Winter, Jane Harvey, Margaret Baxter, Jane Fletcher, Martin Reece, Dianne Fletcher, Christine Baxter, Susan Pridmore, Peter Pridmore, Jeremy Holmes, Stephen Davenport, Judith Exley, Melody Nortcliffe, Julia Chan, Catherine Bullock, Nicole Bennett and Hugh Melville.

Dobcroft Middle School orchestra included nearly seventy musicians when this photograph was taken in 1975, among them Susan Bullock, Erica Middleton, Andrew Sumner, John Stoddart, Margaret Walton, David Beech, Louise Thorpe, Christine Jordan, Simon Harvey, Sarah Fox, Toby Kohler, Andrew Marshall, Vivien Saunders, Catherine Saunders, David Barker, Anna Walker, Mark Wheen, Susan Wragg, Jane Morrell, Deborah Kessell, Belinda Kessell, Andrew Greaves, Melanie Dick, Susan Colley, Ruth Watt and Jane Blank. The conductor, Mrs E.J. Peters, is standing on the left. Anna Walker, second from right on the middle row, went on to become a well-known television personality.

This peaceful rural scene is now a busy dual-carriageway road. The land on the right later became the Beauchief end of Millhouses Park. The boundary wall was set back to widen the road and some of the mature trees were retained on the roadside verge, although there are not so many left now. On the left, next to Ecclesall Woods, trams eventually ran on a reserved track. When the trams stopped running in 1960 the track was taken up and the road became dual carriageway.

All it says on the caption to this photograph is 'Path from Ecclesall Woods, Millhouses'. With no buildings for reference and the path possibly long gone, it is difficult to say now where it was taken. I have included it specially for people who like to ponder such things and come up with ideas of their own.

The old Millhouses church hall at the corner of Dobcroft Road and Whirlowdale Road was opened on 6 October 1928 and for nearly forty years served a variety of purposes: meetings, jumble sales, amateur drama, Boy Scout, Girl Guide and Brownie activities, and home of the local youth club. In the 1960s a new church hall was built between Holy Trinity church and the vicarage and the old hall was taken down.

When the site of the old church hall was cleared a new youth centre was built, slightly higher up Dobcroft Road and nearer to Whirlowdale Road. It opened in 1966 and this photograph was taken soon after the opening.

The outbuildings on the right hand side of the Waggon and Horses were converted into a garage in 1926. From then until about 1956, the garage was owned and run by Arnold Gent. In this 1920s photograph it has four of the old-style petrol pumps with tubs of flowers spaced between them.

In later years new petrol pumps were installed and there were more of them. When Mr Gent left, the garage was taken over by Jack Thompson. He ran it for about ten years then moved the business to Meadowhead. The old garage at the side of the Waggon and Horses was knocked down and replaced by a car park. Mr Gent's son, Mike, was brought up in Millhouses, went into the licensed trade, changed pubs several times and is now back in the area, running the Millhouses Hotel.

Four of the old shops opposite Millhouses post office were demolished in 1976. Just before their closure they were occupied by J.W. Rose, baker, Mail Graphic, Millhouses Fisheries and Millhouses Engineering Company Ltd. The site is now part of the forecourt of a filling station.

The first of the shops on Terminus Road, Millhouses, were built in 1927. Originally there were seven: a Sheffield and Ecclesall Co-operative Society grocery, Edward Beckett, butcher, Wiley and Co. Ltd, wine merchants, Ethel Worrall, newsagent, Elfred Andries, confectioner, Doris Glossop's Hartington Fruit Store and James S. Kingston, confectioner. By the time this picture was taken in the 1930s, four more shops had been added. These were the four on the left with black and white frontages: Albert Swift, pork butcher, Gertrude Mary Daykin, ladies' hairdresser, Horace D. Wragg, grocer and Sarah A. Bennett, draper and ladies' outfitter. Three more shops were added around 1960.

Shopkeepers on Terminus Road, Millhouses, decided to liven things up in the 1980s by holding an annual Festival Week, with competitions, jazz bands, pop groups, children's attractions, displays and so on. John Stacey, of Stacey's grocery stores and Sue Shaw, of Sue's hardware shop, are pictured dressed for the occasion at the May 1989 festival.

Many of the attractions during Millhouses Festival Week were held on the grassed area in front of Terminus Road shops, with crowds standing on the road or sitting on the grassy bank to watch. Now that the site has been built on, scenes like this will be impossible.

The lady standing with her back to the camera, chatting at the soft drinks counter of Millhouses youth centre, is not one of the regulars. It's Princess Margaret. On 15 November 1966 the Princess visited Sheffield and called in at the youth centre which had been completed six months before.

The Revd Arthur Mawson, left, Vicar of Millhouses and chairman of the youth centre management committee, showed the Princess round the new centre on her twenty-five minute visit. She met youth club members and saw displays of photographs of club events.

Youth club leader Derek Doman, third from right, looks on as the Princess chats with club members. About fifty Scouts, Cubs, Guides and Brownies formed up outside as she arrived for her visit, one of three engagements she had that day. She also attended the rehallowing and consecration of the new Chapel of St George at Sheffield Cathedral and she opened Handsworth parish centre's new youth wing.

Three

Millhouses Park

Parts of the old corn mill from which Millhouses gets its name can still be seen today but the old mill dam, seen here in the early 1900s, was filled in long ago. The photograph was taken before Millhouses Park was laid out, looking across what is now the cricket pitch. In the picture there is a cricket match in progress in the distance on what is now the car park. The old corn mill was mentioned in a thirteenth century document. The buildings that remain are used as stores by the Parks Department.

Above: Millhouses Park had not been formally laid out when this photograph was taken in the summer of 1914. The small hut, centre, is still there, at the side of what is now the boating pond and the buildings between the trees, right, are the Waggon and Horses public house and its outbuilding. There is a cricket match going on in the distance, left, on land now covered by housing.

Left: The River Sheaf looks decidedly messy in this picture. As part of the development of Millhouses Park, the river bank was tidied up and walled in various places.

Open Air Bathing Pool, Millhouses. 2.

Above: The photographer who took this picture in the 1930s captured a youngster in blurred mid-flight from the high diving board. The open air pool, which opened on 15 August 1929, was a popular attraction during heatwaves but at other times the water was very cold. It was also very dark which made it difficult to see any swimmer who was in trouble. In 1967 it was announced that the pool would be closed and replaced by a new 'super suntrap lido'. Work on the new lido started the following year.

Right: A scribbled note on the back of this picture postcard says only that the photograph was taken at Millhouses Park. It has a 1930s look about it, but nothing is known about the event or precisely where in the park it took place.

Above: The open air pool had very little grass for sunbathing so swimmers often sat on the edge of the pool, as they are doing on this picture taken in August 1964. Sitting on the edge was not comfortable. The concrete edging stones could be very rough on bare skin.

Left: The River Sheaf runs quite deep alongside the old swimming pool site. It is one of two stretches along the river where paddling and swimming have never been allowed.

Opposite: One of the more spartan traditions at Millhouses Park was practised by a small group of swimmers who went for a dip in the open air pool every year on Christmas Day. They kept up the tradition even if it meant smashing a hole in the ice to reach the water, as it did on Christmas Day, 1950.

THE RIVER, MILLHOUSES, SHEFFIELD.

Fishing for minnows and sticklebacks in the River Sheaf has been one of the juvenile attractions of Millhouses Park probably since the day it opened. These days, however, the fishing has become more serious. There are trout in the river these days.

MILLHOUSES PARK

One of the significant things about this 1938 picture of the bridge across the Sheaf is that the four-bar wooden fence on the left was considered enough in those days to prevent people straying onto the Sheffield–St Pancras railway line. Today, there is a six foot high metal mesh fence and even that is not enough.

The old rustic woodwork on the bridge across the River Sheaf in Millhouses Park was replaced at some time by a more sturdy iron railing. Apart from that, things are still pretty much as they were in this 1938 photograph. The forms on the left bank have gone, the wall on the right bank is not as well preserved, but the bush in the centre is still there nearly sixty years later and the overall view is hardly changed.

Fondly remembered by several generations of bowlers, putters and tennis players, the old sports pavilion in Millhouses Park was badly damaged in April 1983 by a fire in which a man died. Judged to be beyond repair, the pavilion was demolished and, to the dismay of regular users, was replaced by a much less fondly regarded prefab structure near the putting green.

Millhouses Park was badly damaged by heavy flooding on the night of 1 July 1958. The River Sheaf overflowed its banks leaving several inches of mud on bowling greens, smashing the wire fences around tennis courts (above) and leaving rubble all over paths and turf.

The flash flood turned the Sheaf into a torrent so powerful that it smashed down this concrete and stone footbridge near the cricket pitch. The remains were cleared away and the bridge was never rebuilt.

Millhouses lido was opened on 23 May 1970 and although it was essentially a fun pool rather than a serious swimmer's pool, for nearly twenty years it attracted large crowds whenever there was warm weather. The beginning of the end for the lido came in August 1980 when it was closed because the City Council did not have the funds to carry out necessary repairs. The closure became permanent, the funds were still not available and the lido was dismantled and filled in. The site is now level and weed-covered but a band of local residents are busy fundraising with ambitious plans to turn it into a leisure and play area.

Like the lido, the children's paddling pools were a big attraction for many years at Millhouses Park. But again like the lido, they are in need of repairs and the City Council does not have the funds to carry them out, so the pools have been closed. In the hot summers of 1995 and 1996 they were waterless and deserted.

At the bottom end, the children's paddling pools drain into the River Sheaf when necessary. The bridge to the right is part of the path from the playground area, past the pools up to the tennis courts and bowling greens.

MILLHOUSES PARK. SHEFFIELD.

The old open air pool with its diving boards is on the right of this photograph, taken in the 1950s. The disappearance of the pool is not the only obvious change since then. The small conifers scattered about between the flower gardens are now twenty-five or thirty feet high.

The park's boating pool, popular with youngsters and regular venue for model boating competitions, was photographed here in 1969. In 1996, after two years of drought, it too is closed because of the shortage of water. In ancient times there was a corn mill on the site.

Perhaps, as Ratty said, there is absolutely nothing half so much worth doing as messing about in boats, but messing about with them comes close, as these youngsters knew. They were taking part in the children's model boat races on the boating pond at Millhouses Park in June 1967.

Right: During Bob-a-Job Week in April 1969, local Scouts helped to spruce up the boats on Millhouses Park boating pool.

Below: The park has always been known for the beauty of its flower beds but the flowers in this area on the Abbeydale Road South boundary, opposite Pingle Road, were replaced by shrubs in the 1980s.

Photographed against one of their borders in 1974, these were the Millhouses Park staff responsible for the brilliant floral displays and trim lawns. Left to right: Martin Turner, apprentice, Frank Clark, apprentice, Ernest Keen, gardener, Trevor Drew, foreman and Darrell Stent, supervisor.

Even under snow Millhouses Park has its attractions, as this picture, taken after a late snowfall in April 1981, shows. Fortunately it wasn't heavy enough to flatten the tulips.

Four

Beauchief and Beyond

Beauchief corner, around 1905, looking up Abbey Lane towards Beauchief station. The building on the left is the old Beauchief post office at the corner of Abbeydale Road South and Abbey Lane.

Another view of Beauchief corner, this time looking towards what is now Abbeydale Road South. At the time this photograph was taken the hotel on the right was called the Abbeydale Station Hotel. It is better known in modern times as the Beauchief Hotel. Abbey Lane leads off to the right behind the patiently-waiting horse.

The old Beauchief post office was still there and structurally, very much the same in 1961. There's a television aerial on the roof, cars where the carts used to be and the old gas lamp has gone, but the Rowntree's chocolates sign is still there over the window. Not long after this photograph was taken the building was demolished and a filling station was built on the site.

The Beauchief Hotel, formerly the Abbeydale Station Hotel, was well known for its bowling green and the club that played on it. When the bowling green closed in the 1970s and was replaced by a car park, most of the Abbeydale bowlers moved down the road to play at Millhouses Park.

Station Cottage, near the railway bridge at the bottom of Abbey Lane, is seen here in 1904. It was probably built around 1870 for somebody who worked at the newly-opened railway station nearby.

Although it looks slightly different in modern times, the lane leading to Beauchief Abbey from Abbey Lane is still a pleasant walk on a Sunday morning. The tower of the abbey can be seen through the arch of trees on this photograph, taken around 1906, and there are fields all around. Nowadays the abbey seems to be surrounded by golf courses.

Beauchief Abbey, from which Abbeydale gets its name, was founded by Robert Fitz-Ranulph in the twelfth century and dedicated to St Thomas the Martyr. After the Dissolution it was demolished and its stones were used for several local buildings, including Beauchief Hall. All that remains is the Abbey chapel which was built in the seventeenth century. It has been sketched, painted and photographed many times. This early 1900s photograph shows the chapel and nearby cottages before they were surrounded by golf courses and before houses had been built on Abbey Lane, to the left of the picture.

There's an admirable precision about the caption to this picture postcard issued by Morgan and Son. It says: 'Tree struck by lightning at Beauchief, June 23, 1906, 9.30pm'. The captions were often written by Mr Morgan's son, who wasn't very old at the time. He did a good job with this one. The building in the background is Beauchief Abbey.

Beauchief Hall was built by Edward Pegge in 1671 with stones retrieved from the ruins of Beauchief Abbey. It was intended to be a home for his son who was about to be married. The son died before the marriage took place and the hall was left unfinished for 160 years. Once completed, it was for many years the home of the Pegge-Burnell family who were large landowners in the area.

In modern times Beauchief Hall has been a school, a country club and a private house.

Beauchief Abbey chapel can just be seen to the right of this photograph, taken soon after Abbey Lane tram route was opened in April 1927. On land to the left of the picture was a hut that was used during the Second World War by the Local Defence Volunteers, later renamed the Home Guards.

Abbey Lane, as this 1930s photograph shows, was developed as a wide thoroughfare. Higher up it was wide enough for the trams to run along a reserved track, separated from other traffic.

Abbeydale Hall, seen here in 1932, is sometimes referred to in early Directories as Abbeydale Villa, or Abbeydale Park. It was built around 1860 and was the home of John Roberts, silversmith and benefactor. Ebenezer Hall was apprenticed to Mr Roberts, progressed to become his business partner and lived at the hall after Mr Roberts died. For three years in the 1930s, the hall was the headquarters of the old Norton Rural Council. In recent times it has been used by the Sheffield College.

Tyzack, Sons and Turner's Abbeydale Works, pictured here in 1940, were given to Sheffield in 1935 for development as a museum. It was to be another thirty-five years before the museum opened as Abbeydale Industrial Hamlet. In the meantime, the old crucible furnaces at the works were used during the Second World War for steel production. Immediately after the war there was no money for setting up new museums.

Opposite above: Mainly through the efforts of the Council for the Conservation of Sheffield Antiquities and a small group of dedicated enthusiasts, the plan to make Abbeydale Works into a museum survived, and laborious restoration work was carried out in the five years before Abbeydale Hamlet was opened to the public on 30 April 1970. One of the men closely involved in the restoration work was Humphrey Nowill, pictured here on the swing seat of the tilt hammer in 1969.

Opposite below: Open days are held regularly at the Hamlet, often with displays out in the courtyard. When a craftsmen's fair was held there in June 1979, the Lord Conyers Morris Men, from Kiveton Park, near Sheffield, were one of the attractions.

George Dalton explains the working of a crucible furnace to a group of visitors during an Abbeydale Industrial Hamlet open day in March 1981.

Beyond Abbeydale Industrial Hamlet and sandwiched between the main road and the railway line to London, Beauchief Garden forms a quiet little oasis, with its water feature, rockeries and well kept turf. Since this 1940s photograph was taken more trees have grown alongside the railway line. The photographer managed to get a train passing by but he missed the locomotive.

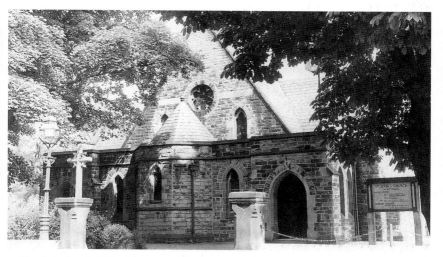

St John's church, Abbeydale, pictured here in 1959, was built by John Roberts of Abbeydale Park and, when it was first built it was in the diocese of Lichfield. It was consecrated in 1876 by the Bishop of Lichfield. A parish room, built in 1893, was paid for by Ebenezer Hall, Mr Roberts' successor at Abbeydale Park.

The Licensed Victuallers' Association almshouses, twelve houses and a boardroom, were built opposite Dore and Totley station in 1879 to replace a group of older almshouses at Grimesthorpe. The Wiley Monument, which was originally at Grimesthorpe, was moved to the new building and can be seen in this Edwardian photograph to the left of the gates. It was erected in memory of Alderman Thomas Wiley, who paid for the almshouses to be built.

Beauchief Singers were started as a ladies' octet by Mrs Esther Mann in 1941, primarily with the aim of raising funds for various charities. The choir grew and sang at concerts all over the area. It was photographed here in 1971 performing a concert version of Edward German's Merrie England, with Mrs Mann conducting. Mrs Mann died the following year and the choir was disbanded after thirty years of fund raising.

Five

Transport

To most of the people who used it, or lived in the area, this was Millhouses station, but when it was first opened, in 1870, it was called Ecclesall station. Later it became Mill Houses and Ecclesall and later still, Millhouses and Ecclesall. In 1903 it was widened and given an island platform. The entrance hall and ticket office were on the first floor of the building on the island platform, at road bridge level.

Millhouses and Ecclesall station seen through one of the arches of the road bridge in 1967. Just over a year later, on 10 June 1968, the station was closed.

After the closure of the station the slow lines to and from Hope Valley were removed, but the platforms and the old station buildings remained for several years. By the 1970s, when this photograph was taken, grass was growing on the once neatly kept platforms.

It was the early 1980s before the station buildings and platforms were removed, although the rubble was still there when this British Rail class 47 passed through on its way south in 1983. By then, building work had started on the new Sainsbury's store to the right. Beyond the building site is the old Laycock Engineering works.

Even small suburban stations like Millhouses had porters in Edwardian times.

Millhouses locomotive sheds opened on 15 April 1901 and for many years housed the passenger locomotives for train services out of Sheffield Midland Station. A Midland compound stands outside on this 1940s photograph. The sheds closed on 31 December 1961 and the building was taken over by a local firm.

An old Midland Railway 0-6-0 steams jauntily past Millhouses locomotive sheds in the early 1900s with a seven coach train it has brought down the Hope Valley line. The main lines between Sheffield and London are the two nearer the camera. The footpath on the far side of the tracks is the path to the loco sheds from Archer Road bridge.

Before 1903, when the station was widened and given an island platform, Beauchief had only two platforms, with no buildings on the up side, as shown here.

At very nearly the same spot, a four-car diesel multiple unit approaches Sheffield in 1976. The changes are obvious. The four lines have been reduced to two. The semaphore signals and the signal box have gone. The locomotive sheds have closed. New buildings have gone up on both sides of the line.

Abbeydale Road-Abbey Lane junction as it was around 1908, with Beauchief and Abbey Dale station (as it was then called) in the foreground, and Abbeydale Station Hotel (later the Beauchief Hotel) at the junction. In recent years the land beyond the station has been developed, and the gap between the houses on Abbey Lane has been filled in with modern bungalows.

A double-headed Midland Railway express blasts out white smoke as it passes through Beauchief station and under Abbey Lane bridge around 1916.

Beauchief station from Abbey Lane bridge in the early 1900s, with a Manchester express approaching. The land behind the station on this photograph has become the site of a new nursing home in the 1990s.

Photographed the day after it closed on 2 January 1961, Beauchief station is deserted but still there. Today there are few signs to show anyone where it was. Platforms and buildings have gone and the entrances from Abbey Lane bridge have been filled in.

Opposite above: When the Midland main line was opened from Sheffield to Chesterfield in 1870, there was no Dore and Totley station. Dore and Totley was an afterthought. The stations at Heeley, Millhouses and Beauchief were built with the new line. Dore and Totley followed two years later, opening on 1 February 1872. A photograph like this, taken around 1904 as a double-headed express was passing through, would be impossible today because of the number of trees that have grown alongside the line.

Opposite below; Opposite: By the late 1960s, when this photograph was taken, Dore and Totley was closed as a main line station. The footbridge had been cut back to the island platform and the buildings on the island platform were boarded up. Since then the footbridge has gone altogether, only the platform on the left is in use – as a diesel halt – and the station building on the left has become a restaurant.

DORE AND TOTLEY STATION

Amazingly, there were no serious injuries to locomotive crews or passengers when a Sheffield to Birmingham and Bristol express crashed at Dore and Totley on 9 October 1907. The train was being hauled by two locomotives and the second ran foul of the points, went off the rails and crashed onto its side, hitting the station platform and smashing off its dome. The driver and fireman were thrown out of the cab and had cuts and bruises. The coaches stayed upright and there were no injuries among the passengers.

The extent of the damage to the derailed locomotive can be seen in this picture, taken after the line had been cleared and the locomotive had been lifted upright.

ABBEY LANE MOTOR SERVICES LTD.

Abbey Lane Motor Service Ltd. started business in December 1930 with a saloon car and a van. By 1937 it had a capital value of £75,000, a fleet of twenty-four luxurious, Sheffield-built coaches, an office in the city centre and a garage at the bottom of Abbey Lane, behind the Beauchief Hotel.

ABBEY LANE MOTOR SERVICES LTD.

Abbey Lane Motor Services' coaches were built by Cravens of Darnall and the quality of the interior design can be seen here: curtained windows, carpeted central walkway, wall clock above the heater on the bulkhead and floral moquette seat covering. The company ran a daily service between Sheffield and Ollerton, known as the Dukeries Service.

In the early days, the only route indicators Sheffield tram cars had, front and rear, were large initial letters. The first trams to run along Abbeydale Road carried the initial letter 'A' for Abbeydale. When the line was extended the letter was changed to 'M' for Millhouses, as displayed here by tram No. 152, photographed near Hastings Road.

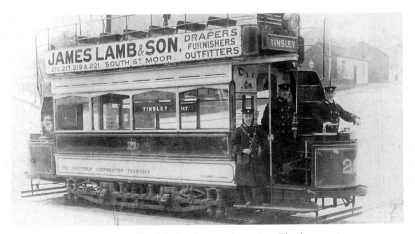

Tramlines progressed along Abbeydale Road section by section. The first terminus was at Woodseats Road. This was extended to Bannerdale Road in 1901, then to Hastings Road in 1902. By the time this photograph was taken the terminus was at the bottom of Millhouses Lane, on the right of this picture.

The old tram terminus at Millhouses Lane is viewed here from the opposite side of the road, with the post office in the background and Archer Road going off to the right.

Like all old tram termini, Millhouses Lane had its long cane pole which the crew used to reverse the overhead trolley ready for the trip back to town. It can be seen hanging on its hook on the standard at the left of the picture. Watching the conductor or driver pulling the trolley off the wire and hauling it round the tram was a popular spectator sport for children.

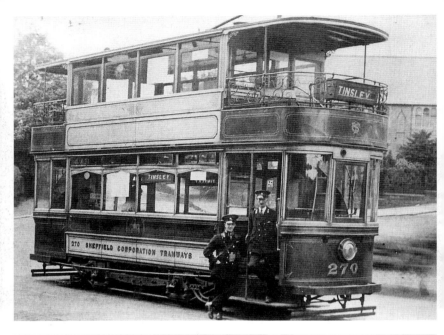

A fine collection of tram cars and crews at Millhouses some time between 1906 and 1908. It's thought that the trams were parked up after taking schoolchildren to Millhouses Park for a special event, possibly Empire Day celebrations. The tram nearest to the camera has a poster in the window which says, 'Abbeydale School'.

Opposite above: Millhouses Lane terminus again, with the Methodist church, right, before it was enlarged, and the crew posing casually before setting off for Tinsley.

Opposite below: There are many different photographs of the Sheffield tram car that was decorated and illuminated for the coronation of King George V in May 1911, but nearly all of them were taken inside Queens Road tram shed. The Transport Department allowed people into the tram shed, on payment of a small fee, to photograph the car. Pictures of it out on the road are much harder to find. This one was taken on Abbeydale Road, near the end of Bannerdale Road.

Sheffield's first covered top tram cars were built by Sheffield Corporation in 1905, but as this picture, taken on Abbeydale Road, shows, while the upper deck was covered the driver, the conductor and the staircases at either end were still open to the elements.

Opposite above: Snow plough tram No. 274 at work on Abbeydale Road on 1 April 1917. The sign on the shop to the left says, 'Jas. Coombes and Co., Boot Repairing Factory. Over 150 branches'. No. 274, a converted horse car, remained in service till 1952.

Opposite below: At one stage, when Sheffield's tram routes were being extended to the outer suburbs, there was a suggestion that the Millhouses route should be taken as far as Totley. This never happened. It was, however, extended to Beauchief corner, seen here in the 1930s, and up Abbey Lane, on the right of the picture, to link up with Woodseats route.

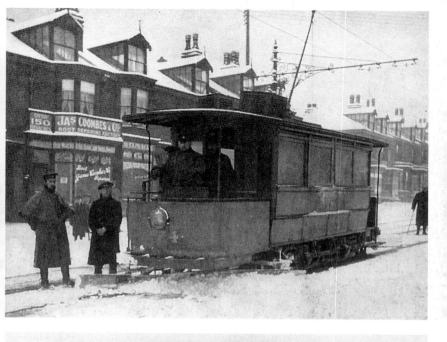

Abbeydale Rd. South, Beauchief, Sheffield

Tram cars had to lean into the sharp bend at Abbey Lane corner; their wheels tended to squeal rather a lot round the curve.

When the tram route was extended from Millhouses Lane to the Waggon and Horses in 1926, a turning loop was built so that trams did not have to reverse. It was the only one of its kind in the city and it was a favourite spot for tram photographers. The subject in this case was tram No. 501, a revolutionary new design built by Sheffield Transport Department at their Queens Road works and introduced in 1946. Another thirty-five were built by Charles Robert and Co. They were the last new design before the trams were abandoned in 1960.

After the Abbey Lane tram route closed on 28 February 1959, Beauchief became the terminus. Tram No. 264, pictured here at Beauchief, is about to reverse. The arrangement did not last long. Less than two years later Sheffield's trams stopped running and the city switched over to buses. The finale of the Last Tram Week celebrations on 8 October 1960 was a procession of fifteen trams to Beauchief, then back through the city centre to Tinsley. Despite pouring rain, thousands of people turned out to watch.

When Millhouses tram terminus was at the bottom of Millhouses Lane, the area in front of the Robin Hood Hotel became the accepted place for country buses to wait. There are three in this photograph, Charles Battey's bus for Baslow and Bakewell, left, Newsome's bus for Holmesfield, centre, and a Sheffield open top double decker for Totley, right. Newsome was a local operator based in Abbeydale Road. The Corporation bus service to Totley started in 1914.

Another picture of the area in front of the Robin Hood Hotel in the days when it was a busy bus terminus. Sheffield Transport Department's solid-tyred double decker carries the route number 45, the original number of the service from Millhouses to Totley. The return journey from Totley was route 44.

The clatter of an old stage coach returned to Abbeydale Road in 1905 and 1906. At holiday times coach proprietor Reuben Thompson ran his 'Old Times' coaches on day trips from Sheffield to Baslow and Bakewell via Froggatt Edge. The coaches, one of which is seen here at Baslow, were very popular when the weather was good.

Six

Firms and Businesses

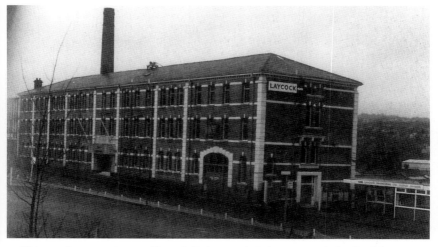

This was what passers-by saw of Laycock Engineering Ltd, the imposing Archer Road frontage, with its main entrance to the reception area halfway along. For a while after the building was demolished in 1996 the front step of the entrance was the only thing left in place, but even that has now gone.

Laycock Engineering were the largest employers in the Abbeydale and Millhouses area. In their heyday about 2,500 people worked there, and this 1940s aerial view shows how large their factory was. Except for the brickworks on the right, and the dairy and a few other buildings on the left, Laycocks occupied all the land between Archer Road and the railway. Now the works have gone. In the early 1990s the firm closed and most of the buildings were demolished. The four storey office block was last to go, in 1996, and at the time of writing the site was being prepared for a large new development, including an extension to Sainsbury's store and a new leisure centre.

There was no thought of closure when this photograph was taken of some of the forge workers at Laycock Engineering in about 1950. Unfortunately the caption gives only surnames for most of the group and it isn't clear who is where on the picture. The names given are: Broadhead, O'Connor, Rowe, Dickinson and Revill; J. Hadfield, McCall, Carter, Johnson, Cooney and F. Smith; Cartwright, Young and Gordon.

Members of Laycocks Inspection Staff enjoying a Christmas party in the 1940s.

Laycock employees on an outing to London in the 1950s.

Laycock Engineering moved to the Millhouses site in 1901. Although they started out making railway equipment and fittings, the firm soon diversified, produced a lorry, the Laycock Goodchild, aircraft engines and, after the First World War, a motor car, the Charron Laycock, produced in co-operation with the French car manufacturer, Charron. Several different types were made and one them, carefully restored, was preserved and on show in the firm's reception area. Raymond Morris, who worked for the company for fifty-one years, is seen here showing the car to his three-year-old grandson, Ian, in the 1980s.

C.E. Richardson and Co. Ltd, of Finbat Works, Aizlewood Road, made motor cars between 1919 and 1921, concentrating on a cheap, light car with a two-seat open body and a dicky seat at the back. It sold reasonably well but the company collapsed in 1921. This preserved and restored example of the Richardson car is in Kelham Island Industrial Museum, Sheffield.

Abbey Glen Laundry, Coniston Road, started in a very small way when Agnes Youle went out one November morning in 1900 with a wickerwork trolley and a list of potential customers. The list she made ninety-six years ago is still in the firm's archives, carefully preserved, and the original wickerwork trolley has pride of place in the reception area. Mrs Youle and her husband, Albert, built up the business so well that within six years they moved into the large Coniston Road premises. The firm is still flourishing and still in the same family. The chairman, David Sempers, is a grandson of Mr and Mrs Youle and his son, Tim Sempers, is managing director.

Snowite Ltd, another Abbeydale laundry business, was based in Barmouth Road and this picture, from the 1930s, shows Snowite's flat pack department, where the girls worked on sheets and pillowcases. The two on the right, with sewing machines, repaired any tears in the linen. Snowite was eventually taken over by the Abbey Glen Laundry, one of several acquisitions by Abbey Glen. The others included the Worksop Laundry and part of the old established Clarks of Retford business.

A busy laundry needs its transport and in the early days, that meant a fleet of horse-drawn vehicles, seen here lined up on Coniston Road.

One of Abbey Glen's earliest motor vans.

The early, solid-tyred van is on the far right of this photograph, but the more up-to-date and smartly turned out Albion vehicles take precedence nearer to the camera.

By the 1930s Abbey Glen was still using Albion vehicles, but much sleeker and larger models; it had also expanded its area with premises in Wellgate, Rotherham.

Above: Abbey Glen Laundry staff, including Olive Gresham, right, and Betty Wragg, centre, met members of the touring West Indies cricket team at Queen's Park, Chesterfield, in July 1980, when the West Indies played Derbyshire. Abbey Glen handled the tourists' laundry during the visit.

Right: Loxleys, the printers and stationers, are associated in the collective Sheffield memory with Fargate in the city centre. The business was started there by the Loxley Brothers, William and Edward in 1854 and there was a Loxleys shop in Fargate, although in different premises, for more than one hundred years. The best remembered was probably this one at No. 57. For more than seventy years however, the firm's works have been at Aizlewood Road, off Abbeydale Road.

Loxleys ceased to be a family firm when William Loxley sold it in 1911, but it kept the old name and flourished so well that by 1920 larger premises were needed. What had previously been the Empire Roller Skating Rink in Aizlewood Road proved ideal and the firm moved into the old rink in June 1921. Less than three years later, on 6 December 1923, the building was gutted by a mystery fire, the effects of which can be seen on this photograph taken next morning.

Opposite above: When the Aizlewood Road factory was rebuilt the architect was told to retain the somewhat ornate frontage of the old roller skating rink and when it was completed the new building looked exactly like the old one, but had a slightly different roof. The new premises opened in August 1925. Although there have been extensions, the main building still looks the same in the 1990s.

Opposite below: Opposite: In the early 1960s compositors like these were still setting metal type, in what the trade calls letterpress printing. Loxleys were one of the first commercial printers to go over to litho printing and, with new technology, no type setting is done in the works at all now. Most of the setting is done by the customers and arrives at the firm on computer disk.

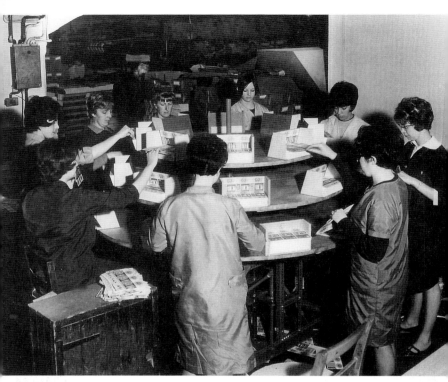

For many years Loxleys have done printing work for a wide variety of national concerns. The staff photographed here around 1960, were working on promotional coupons for Omo soap powder on a collating carousel devised by one of the firm's own engineers. Three revolving tiers avoided the staff having to walk about to fetch the sheets they needed. The ladies in the picture are: Pat Cantril, Pat Hunt, Sylvia Cartledge, Janet Llewelyn, Vicky Ashmore, Hazel Parkinson, Margaret Whiteley, Pauline Digby and Irene Blackshaw.

Seven

Sport

The MCC – Millhouses Cricket Club – has one of the loveliest grounds in Yorkshire. Set amid trees at the eastern end of Millhouses Park, its only minor drawback is the nearness of the River Sheaf on one boundary which means that a long pole has to be kept handy on match days to retrieve big hits from the river. The Millhouses team around 1946 was, back row, left to right: Ken Mills, Rex Hardy, Albert Hinchliffe, George Greaves, Reg Pashley, Cyril Hibbert (umpire); front, left to right: Mr Oversby (scorer), Horace Staniforth, John Tasker, Dave Farrand, Sid Thompson, Ted Shaw. The little boy was the son of one of the players.

Large crowds turned out to see a Millhouses Thursday team play T. Brown's Mexborough XI at cricket on 3 June 1909. The man they had come to see was one of the Mexborough team, James William 'Iron' Hague, who earlier in the year had become Heavyweight Boxing Champion of England by beating Gunner Moir at the National Sporting Club. He did less well on the cricket field. He was clean bowled for a duck.

When Sheffield United decided to rebuild their Bramall Lane ground in 1973 and do away with the cricket pitch, Yorkshire County Cricket Club had to look for a new ground for their Sheffield matches. They chose Abbeydale Park, photographed here during a county match in July 1976. Now, county matches look like becoming a thing of the past. It was announced in 1996 that Yorkshire would no longer play at Sheffield, the city where the club was founded in 1863.

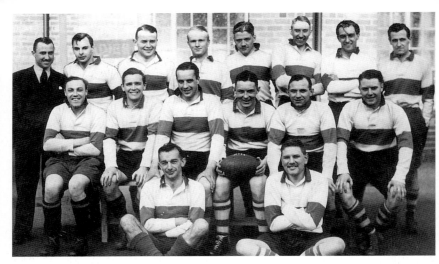

Abbeydale Park is also the home of many other sporting organisations, among them, Sheffield Rugby Union Football Club. This team picture was taken in April 1939 when they beat a Rest of Sheffield XV in a match in aid of the *Sheffield Telegraph* Children's Seaside Holiday Fund. Back row, left to right: K. George, president, R. Greenham, G. Greaves, M. Colver, C. Dearnley, P.V. Avis, H. Marsden, W.M. Hutchinson; front row: F. Shepley, J. Hargreaves, G.C. Watson, D. Joy, G.A. Allen, G. Francis; seated: W. Rees and M. Stride.

Sheffield Ladies Hockey Club squad photographed at Abbeydale Park in September 1987. Back row, left to right: Carol Sharman, Helen Giorgi, Marie Courtney, Jane Shaw, Pat Whitaker, Tina Bradshaw, Judy Williams, Sue Moroney, Elaine Burt, Maureen Leighfield, Jane Veys; front: Margo Mazur, Lesley Sharman, Sarah Stocks, Sheila Bell, Lesley Gardiner, Julie Binney, Barbara Cooke, Meg Guest, Jo Beresford, Hazel Broadbent.

Abbey Glen Laundry football team photographed in the 1940s.

The Waggon and Horses football team, pictured in 1974, played in the Sunday Sports League. Their home ground was at Castle Dyke, Ringinglow Road. Standing, left to right: Steve Cadman, Steve Hodgson, Brian Carr, Phil Power, Chris Gebhardt, Bob Brown; front, left to right: Gordon Taylor, Dave Colley, Billy Clarke, John Harrod, Richard Oldfield.

Abbeydale Bowling Club, photographed around 1955. Back row, left to right: F. Quixall, W. Brentnall, W.H. Birch, M. Rowland, F. Thompson, R.H. Jackson, L. Cooper, G.H. Jackson; front, left to right: Mrs A. Barton, Mrs B. Ashley, Mrs A. Yeardley, Mrs F. Quixall, Mrs M. Rowland, Mrs G.H. Jackson, Mrs L. Cooper, Mrs E. Cowsill.

Millhouses Park Ladies' Bowling team won the Justice Burdall League in 1963 with an impressive record: played 16, won 15, drawn 1. Points for, 2,183; points against, 1,643. Back row, left to right: Mary Jackson, Madge English, Rose Cox, Gladys Bolton, Gladys Ross, Joan Pogmore; front, left to right: Mrs E. Prest, Mrs A. Payne, Winnie Hall (captain), Mrs Clara Withey, Eveline Farr.

Millhouses Park Bowling Club team, photographed in 1980, 'the year they won everything': the Sheffield championship, the Yorkshire championship and, proudest of all, the British championship. Posing behind their collection of silverware are, back row, left to right: Peter Smith, Ian Ross, Duncan Ross, David Hallam, Howard Alcock, Lou Ashforth, Brian Clarke; front row, left to right: Dennis Brannan, Bob Jackson, Brian Drew (captain), Jack Manterfield (club chairman), Gilbert Ross, John Greensmith.

Above: It was trophy presentation night at Millhouses Park Bowling Club when this picture was taken either in the late 1930s or early 1940s. Standing, left to right: Harry Mitchell, Harry Storemont, Mrs Richards, W. Fox, Mrs Dunham, Tom Seaton, Nelson Withey, Steve Pentecost, Frank Calvert, J.C. Cowley, Justice Burdall, Irwin Mitchell, Bill Roberts, Mrs Withey, Jack Manterfield, Arthur Manterfield, George Laister, Walter Bacon; seated, left to right: Mrs Fox, Mrs Eccles, Mrs Beardsley, Louis Everiss. Mr Everiss was bowls correspondent for *The Star* and *Green 'Un* at the time.

Below: Mr Walter Sykes, of Bannerdale Road, was the oldest league bowls player in Sheffield in 1978 at the age of 90. At the other end of the age spectrum, Millhouses Park club runs weekly bowls sessions for youngsters and gets a good turnout for them.

Laycock Engineering tennis team, *c.* 1950: K. Godson, E. Chappell, E. Edwards, E. Renshaw, L. Lambert, R. Wilson.

Laycock Engineering tennis club members photographed on a night out in the 1950s.

Grove Tennis Club, first called Millhouses Lawn Tennis Club, were members of the Sheffield and District Lawn Tennis Association in the early 1900s. They were the first club in the city to install floodlights and had the first all-weather courts in 1970. By 1985 the original all-weather courts needed resurfacing. Seen here cutting the ribbon at the opening of the newly-laid surface in June 1986, are Mrs Wendy Tomlinson and Derek Cave, flanked by Martin Dunstan, left, and Dr Rod Nicholson.

Beauchief municipal golf course club house, photographed in 1959. Originally the home of Abbeydale Golf Club, Beauchief opened as a muncipal course, with a new name, on 10 July 1924.

The club house at Abbeydale Golf Club has an impressive moorland backdrop in this 1967 picture. The club house was built in 1924 when the club moved to its new course.

Abbeydale Golf Club celebrated its centenary in 1995 and to mark the event a commemorative stone was unveiled by Tim Jackson, club captain, seen here, left, with Don Watt-Smith, president of the club. The celebrations included nine days of tournament play and entertainment.

PRICE 2d.

SHEFFIELD'S GREATEST CHARITY GALA

ABBEYDALE PARK

FROM BANK HOLIDAY MONDAY, AUG. 1ST, TO SATURDAY, AUG. 6TH, 1932

ELECTRICITY

for

EASY HOUSEKEEPING

NO SMOKE, DIRT, DUST OR FUMES

CITY of SHEFFIELD ELECTRIC SUPPLY DEPT.
OFFICES & SHOWROOMS ——— COMMERCIAL STREET.

Abbeydale Park was a favourite spot for galas and special events. This charity gala in August 1932 featured an athletics meeting, a medieval ox roasting, a boxing programme organised by Gus Platts, Charles Dudley's Midget Gladiators, a variety show, fireworks and a fair.